M000248878

Untitled Series: Life as It Is

Also by Norman Fischer

Norman Fischer

Untitled Series: Life as It Is

Talisman House, Publishers
Northfield, Massachusetts • 2018

Published in the United States of America by
Talisman House, Publishers
P.O. Box 102
Northfield, Massachusetts 01360

11 12 13 7 6 5 4 3 2 1 First Edition

Manufactured in the United States of America

ISBN: 978-1-58498-133-6

author photo: Noah Fischer.

Man thinking but
Great works when he
Not calculating & thinking
Has to be restored
Long training in of the
Self-forgetfulness
Attained man yet
Not think, thinks
Showers down
Sky-like
Down ocean
Thinks stars
Mighty heavens
Thinks like
Shooting relaxing
Breeze he
Showers oceans
Stars foliage

———

Because
Was ready
Was showing
Two performers
Heard said
Door so
There there
But start till
Later so late
Us with green
There only
Younger read
A little too
Patter he
Announced patter
Good patter
Skillful witty
Significant maybe

———

A few days
Listening crows caw
Three, six, never
Four, five, once
Crows caw only
Times, never more
Last went
One held
Apartment had
Put on there's
No other for
Events on down
In the flats
Of young
This was with maybe
More people living wanted

––––––

With my part
Read the
Sit with
Talk on
More musing
Expression with
This time (due to
I did
Part people
Express poetically
By in much
Time-frame &

———

When she
By now
Ambitious they've
With other
Rent huge
Where I'll
Ten minutes the
Weekend
That night was
Last film
That is he
Now being
But it
As all his
Of ocean, landscape
Double which
Can't with
Dolphins swimming
Cliffs seacoast
Was particularly

———

Yesterday for "Poet"
As show on
Place near shore
Where I used in
So before to
As nursery
Three young people
The show they all got
Copies & had
Good about that
Sunny, pleasant, quiet
Part good the
Hour quickly I
Quite a few poems
Now to in
Finishing Zen
Time, then not

———

About this about
She was against
Was no good
Too talky &
She was a, it was
This all might
In part but
Anyway to take
That way & work too
Her a big
For of but
To print all
Out led to telling
Me put her &
Her down in
Which is also
True & came

———

End of a day
Alone out her
Among her
Many projects &
Which usually
Her & puts
Her in anyway
A while of her
Terrible behavior a
Her not dealing with
In the way
Made & went
To read
Hebrew mystical
Poetry mystical
It's because I

———

Nothing about this
Important but
Writing is typical
Stuff still
Got up & couldn't
To so read
Few more
A job with
Services — no
Of and be
Good to prayers
Though a bit
Too &
Not we
Never stop
This is the
It takes

———

To get
Over it
But good
As always possibly
This too much
Was for me
Had maybe from
Lack of(in
Says he off
For the before
Spare this.
A that moved
Maybe in my
State the two
He starts with
Very slow &

———

Mournful turns to
A song "Dance"
To the by
Once, a cat
The second time
Sings the he
One a woman
Second once, once
A wife in
The third very
Some & some
How not
Was again
Not what we
About beheadings
& this is how
All make preparations

———

For own burial
In fact this
Because doesn't
Should be buried
The with
Her — she's both
Suppose by the
Of being buried
Which she somehow
Is more than
Buried to ask!
The before was
Last in high
We did hit
Walking outside
Talking out loud

———

Practice)I
Was to speak
Out my most
That I will feel
Of for the rest
Life that I'll be
Able for though
Do my early
Self & sexual
Also my to
Blowing up my
Life if need be
Afterward & wanted
To again we'd
A week about
Outburst & her

―――――

"Better life" how
Which sent
Into an about
How, yes, had
Been somehow &
That she had
Terrible afflicting
On her (& on
I have gone
With going to
School &
When had
Done that to him
Seriously beside
With remorse &

———

Pain — exactly
This time of
Many of them
— If differently — had
During the
Well this she wanted
Me that it
Of this — her life
With a it
Really was the
Made it out
& that she
Such a this
Time with a
All the good

———

She had good
For her
She did — I
Had this — that
It was that
Put two large
Up on the
A Huge Book on
Opened. The book
& the book
This was only he
It was the
His with he
Was for that
Though I can't

———

The time — at what
In the saga
The High fell
All this
Was over the other
Overnight & we had
Together in the
Morning. She's
Again (lost her
At the last
Was damaged
Have lived more
A few, had
To be quite
Conversation mashed
The powerful
& energies that

———

Course though she's
A very aware
Person & yet
The same least
To me it's
There's so more
On than ever
On the — that she
May or not know
Me — or am
Making it impossible
Anyway, what does
All this
Name, name, name, etc.
Me of the

———

Blind & loving
& influence that
Are in us by
Practice, yearning
Which are in
Of the in
Book, that I
Feel as I
Of the (while
Sleep-inducing
Of bourbon
Walking on on
Today being
& night
Radio show

———

I discovered I'd
Parted in extra
Of the same
So I but
Of them were
Copies in the
Several repeated
Working on them
In their several
I finally realized some
I had to
& figure out
Was & cut
It all in
Case there is

———

A process
& that took
Difficult hours
Now down to words
Again the words
Lost on
& not as
Expecting (from words
Thought I
But in fact
Have three more
Of to
Which start
& go on
Till giants at

_____

I'd heard
From in they
Were zero then
Came & said
So I got
To hear the
& instead to
Astonishment was
Still on in
On a belt
& shut
In bottom to
Seal it longest
For)history

———

This is the
Me on year
Odd how
Writing is
The other antique
Me from his
This one same
They lost
Their chance
At, on a
Throwing away
At a run
Hear the
But lost they did
& the

———

I listened
I made
& on with
She was a
Now I've
Been emailing
Poet publisher
Her as they
Been but
All over now
To me
Next after
Her emotional entanglement
Me) over her about
Meantime is
Emailing me with
Up about how

―――――

She wants
How she
Thinks should
Change then
Me that is
Down over the
Problem (still) &
How she is
At & her
To an &
That I of this
Is not me
About it
This is a
For me — I do
About all these
Including)being

———

Happy & me
In the of it
All (& being
Of it
Criss-crossing in
The human long
For that
Gets &
In a ways
— & —
Have to with
All of this I
I can it is on
Because today
Dishes the dish rack

———

That the sink
Fell down a
& I got
So yes, I'm this
Can't people me
Alone! (I sound
&, come to
Where is or
When I
Is though that
About this stuff
Can talk
But not
This
& all
Go back to poetry

———

Nobody or
Pays to
Writing of
Words on the
Good but won
Who actually about
Stuff, stuff
About in
To questions
An odd & I'm
Surprised
Accepted the
They just books
Out & don't
Or like me
Also, reading

———

Book, very
I think not
Just the
Stuff that write
He is me
Poets are he
To have lunch
With &
Last night long
About brain
& all the bad
Seem more likely
He knew from
Didn't
Sound impressed

———

More writing
I hate this
Temporary for
An email
Call with rose
Subject said
Research &
My eyes are
Out from — at the
But almost the
I on the
The book the
But that's not
There's a white
Feeling of in
Any text (this

———

The less there's
Intention in the
For a purpose
There even then
Because an
Thrill in) But as
Over the again & again
The words are
That have
Somehow them
Less this
As a text
He & one's then
Meaning in it for
The apparent
Meaning of the
Back to
Reason

———

Read her which more
Explains &
All this in for
The school
I only have &
Probably mostly the
Will get to
On the book
For me was
In reason & love
Sending me more
About her being
About not being
Appreciated &
I guess as
When we about
Of the world it's ourselves

———

Worried about true
I think I told
Down, frustrated, over
But over
At lunch at my
Talk she's
Managing economically
Know how it was
To be the two
Invited &
Has always been
Dark. Yes. Me too.
To me why
To feel dark
Why to be happy
Really the difference
Isn't darkness

———

About darkness really about
That one feel
Differently than me
That feeling this way
Feeling that way
The Difference
One feels — one's always
Got to feel
These short I'm
Out of the
Are interesting because
Bits of language that
Describe feelings of
& then
<u>As being</u>
Salient the content

———

Which is more
The fact of
IN language & out — is
More than our
There are always
There are no
More
This to myself
All my interventions
Words deeds amount
I feel about
This (as I
I'd (or
Matter what my
& level of
Were. Anybody's
Are away in
A moment — the more

———

& the more
One is — &
But the fact of
For a while
With that as
One can is
Always
How one
What one
Does or done
How is is
As in what's
Done and Done
How is one
What all one
Does or Is
As in what's
Done is Done
Isn't what

———

Despair. Yes
To up with
To continue on into
I'm not that
I'm almost anything
I'm over it
Good, nothing
About or for
There might have
At one (bright
But in my
Now all &
Should they
It wouldn't matter

———

Now, never
The of the
All thought
To its is that
Nothing up to
Everything on the
Of its & not
Else. My early
Through all
All meaning
Which is
In a limit
& I'm out with
The fantasy that
Anything at all
Happily achieved

———

On the poetry's
Hope & I've
A couple up
Writing from
Into
Longish &
One short (all
If so &
That seem to me
All right then
Who he'll
It & I
His reading
He wants
In return

———

He probably really does
He's a poet's
Rails against
Pathological
My leftist ideology
Real &
Came with a poem
"This is what I
To talk about"
Funny list of one of
Was how I sighed
Each talk & when
I ever I do
I had a rest
I usually get
— what
About two in

———

Brooklyn the &
& shopping but it
Feel. Am
Maybe bone
I'll never
Anyway, what's a
Problem where there
Other people involved
One's self. I think
Level me too
Probably doing with
But, as I
(That can't be
Her... , I'm sure
Another less exotic
Why is feeling good

———

Better preferred
Why not what's wrong
With … , that is
Mind it
Continue to gripe
My prospects for
Poetry, why
But quickly realize
Had at anyone from
Hardly out work
My books & anyway
Actually to rise
Above my as a minor
In a corner
Works, I feel
Apt expression of
I've done, it's just

———

More would feel
Feel worse, false
& express a
At any utter
Lack & the
Of solitary lonely
Ah, & I don't
About poetry it's so effete!
Like poets on poetry I'm
Something else
My back hurts
All the time

———

The previous
Was 1946
Pretty smoothly
This one's fine
Woke with a
Dream wanted to
It before before I
We were someplace
Maybe hippie crash
It wasn't the old days
It was (vague sense
Large flowing ... , other people
Around remembered now)
Of dream was
Her saying "I don't
& saying it in a sensitive
With usual
Semi-bravado but
At the not

———

Or hurt … , which was
"It's too cheery"
"Well it's
But cheery — the later
But maybe you
Those " [Assume
Much of my
1980's] I mind
Much. I said "But
It's so free to
Press everything, anything"
Which is true.
Impresses me (impresses
Me) for her sense
I guess voice
Very old-fashioned
Writers (& I!)
To destroy that however

———

Much we've tried to
It. Even if
Still somehow
A of how
Sounds characteristically
& if it to
Me I somehow love
In dream she
But softly darkly
Pure & beautiful
& tense & anxious
As old or older
Her years will see her
Later this I
At her
End at I'm
To be with her
With her
Last time

———

A year later, later than that?
Photo then, she
Her saying in
She had to out of
Horrible politics
Yes it's true
So nasty & brutal
& absolutely never
The people its
Beginning with the first
— as if "we"
& right & were only
For their own good
The next terrible war
Following a previous
Of male domination
Rational, cold
Of view

———

Going out to sit
To write this
In a few hours
Later I realized
That maybe it's true
Even the later darker
Maybe despite
The gloom & doom
100 per cent
A cheeriness, I always
To create is inherently
Cheery, art redeems
But this is true
Breezy, cheery
Attitude that's
Never & that always
& around her darkest
She remains always
Undefeated & her poems
Weapon revenge

———

Nightmare dreams converse with her
She's an adamant intimate she's darkly
Soft & lovely but in the dream's not
What I thought howsoever there's always
A swerve, a turn, however you want to
Say it saying it's the point after all
Sad strange beautiful love these simple
Words belie that I've reached for
See long boney wrist out there looking
Out through eyes this isn't phil-
Osophical anyway anymore there's
Just that strain to express to urge
Out to blackest air that then
Dissipates wind blown to a trickle
Right here on a dime at the end

———

Down & back
I gave a
Event at ... , for
For people
Who are going
In care
My is useful
Which is a
In the mind
Field.
Are a goldmine.
That's how
A crook
Enough money never
Again — on fake
After the war

———

So he could over
Well these
Are much better
Still I can't
Get over my
About!
A little earlier
& had with
& his life
Me up at
Me to his
A glass
Walking to load
Which,
We talked
About early days
Memory funnel

———

Story — we to a
By the
(I've
Only who was
A speech that
Mad but I
Indicated sitting next
To me that
That what he
Though I didn't
At all — & this
I have no
Of this &
That I'd been
At the time.
Like, reflected
Memory, I was

———

Made a big
Though I don't
Of that or in the past
Was possessed
By spirit of
Seized me & made
Use of me for a while.
Said he went back to
Of the that I
By how good the
Actual writing was
Would not have
To me now in memory
That I was a little
Top, etc. All
I think of &
My time as not

―――――

I've entirely lost
Materially, emotionally
That part of my
Profoundly, another person
But have kept up with
It & consider it
& experience
Than for me
— my equivalent goes
To, that me
As them
A storyteller
Witty, intensely
& he's &
He said
A faithful Catholic

———

& soon was educated out of
Terribly disillusioned
At having been
& still
It. I hadn't
That the of us
Also fact of having been
Very early (though
I wasn't actually
To — they didn't
Know this & the conversation
So quickly I
To tell them
Those early marriages
Fail just because
Of but

———

(whom I didn't
At all) slept around
(Had an affair
With among
& feeling of being
Betrayed is also close
To & raw &
Rhymes with about
The Church. Makes for a kind
— the original
Of the good, the
Which turns out
To have been a, so
Any faith in goodness, etc.
Is always a gift & a girl
On the street

———

Money to as he
Jesus!" Pisses him off
For a week & he
As if he were still
About it. But he's
Kind & open, loves
Admires — on the sly — so she won't
Who to the
Talk, trim
With fright —
& perfect
In an face
He up with
Spoke at his
To see me

———

[who I learned
Died after said they had been
Since they were
Kids] also keeps
Their soldier who
About war & related
His face behind screen
Son, a street
Addict who's
The people in the street
Have that
Asked about
All she can about
He went by too quickly
Works all the time

———

Find out how. He'd surfaced
When I was at
Somehow found out
"Grow up!" I guess mother
Desperation, he'd
Somehow thinking
But what
And lost
Too, whom he'd
Liked in the first instance
She was a & a
Woman.Woman.
Several of the black
Guys had died
& writing
Bad business to be a strategy for
Decided to & now

———

Leads his own
I can't
& is busy
She should write a letter
He always me
With his
(That he still) steady
Not too or
But. He & his (both
Key questions a bit today
To it, notes
& told me
For an apple to fix. Probably
Of relevance to the acting
Teaching.
Me a of a
Movie that was winter

———

In late starring
About a priest
Who & has the
Dream about a writing conference
Of proving or
Miracles is defeating them
I think. He's doing this
& falls in with who's
Should only be about
Of the miracles. Based on
No doubt miracles a
For to contemplate
Vague faith issues. The story. Meant to
As it in a while
Angry but too watching then

———

The state the personal state
(Very close) &
Left hanging between
Home and going out
At with an
To be carried
Over to of next day
Is stabbing to death
Her lover is optimist for sure
At end of desperate again
Really interesting to
Bitterness & frozenness
You see in person's
Body) is
All too, &, from
Of, can be, should

———

Like an
He'll be so much happier
When he
But I'm sure
Not of view he's
Slammed for it
With his, it's the
Of his &
Which I think
Is true. And he does
A life, myself right away
Good
Who are
Well, a lot for
Has made a lot for
Lookin forward to it
In very nice
With, oddly,

———

Turkish rug
& also
Lots of
The definition of
(Or any other
Is social — that is
Your life in the society you
In is decidedly
The case with. So
See that from
Of view the sweet nice
A kind of
In cahoots with
& cooked —
So he's
Plenty to about
Be to more

———

Time with him
Night, after
Talk, after
With the in the
Went out
To with &
Also did a day
For the
Same day
So was astonished
There was anyone left over
— but —
There were
From was as was
But from that again

_____

Center).
Was funny
Like an awkward
With in
Booth of
Funny & borderline
Lovey remarks
That seemed not 100%
To this
Me but
& in some
Way emotionally
Though he's
& a very
Smart .....still
From

———

So if I had gone there
Maybe
Had but
Because of the
During which
One year I read
I'd've known
I made
But no, it was a
Stupid
& he was
Thinking of grandma. So I guess
It would
Have made no difference
Obviously
& even she

———

Comes across, to be, &
On some it seems sincere
Not important
What she appreciates
She said is
Writing. Maybe she's
That I don't
Don't — & that
In her long years
Her how she is waiting
Had, she said
Which seems
True, she wears as
Her, though it's
Not at all

———

A great edit of
"All right then. If
He did some
Give me a clue
About how
To
Back & did
On other they
Needed it. Now
Work on my
For this
Some notes
On & other
Grandfathers again
In reading it
That you're inside

———

Makes — but
Of language &
Thought (as she
Her) — so it's hard to
Makes you realize how
Makes you want to
So is
Reason entertaining? Yes
But word by word
Yet begun
Time — no more — but I
None of that
Much before
If before
I had to take a breath. If
You "your
Yes -- you get
What you take
Normal or real is called a word
— impossibility of
World as is is

———

You find yourself in
First & second
"Quotes" re this
Look up
Whose book of
Is cited by in
A glove with a false hand
The more or lack
A woman took this up
& to earn a
Suit for a false body
She was a so was
& wrote
For people
Of women in a book
Of women with books
A book
Women then she says she

———

That all authors
Wrote of the
Of women so though she
Had not seen this
She felt she had not noticed
To believe those who
Appreciated shock of soft hair
Words
Were so much wiser
Then she to build
& rooms etc. later in addendum to dream
To overthrow
Woven through the centuries
The false view
Of women they made. She was in
Rectitude words, Justice, Reason
Was to help with
At the table — not mine —
Have another

———

Most & walls — which
Excavations
Would carry out dirt
To build these walls & moat
Dirt being farmer
Views
The shoes that might have been mine
Against women written
With some musical training a pair
With the spade of intelligence
Was a master of
Great facility in
Virtue with a gush of words in
Writing

———

"With the of
Time & universal time
Mark is made
Poetry & poetic
However is marked
By its fluttering between the true
Then what is real
Time is then the
Of the passage from
The True to the Real & back
What allows the
To taste both worlds
This fluttering the
True & the Real is a
Deeper beyond
That form of
Is called

———

About time attempts
In nick of
Flow of time using
Trying
To define
Using
Are probably
Enticing
In study of time
Mysterious flux
More than anything
The deepest of
Enigmas — the nature
Of the self.   Until I
Firm understanding of
Flow of time
Evidence that
An illusion, then I
Will not know who I am
Or what
Great part
In the

———

The trial on my
Phone
At a quarry at the end
By two cheerful normal
But light in tone
— tone —
And feel deserving of that special status
That's
Genius & strangeness
The text — & precise what's casually made
On this & that
Hobnob with luminaries
Outside the gate who keeps guard
Your life
His life
Spent on yours

———

Your prisoner
At end that the
Gate is only for you but you
Go in
In the cathedral by
The station that must have been
— this is the
Just before
Then
Tells him the
Refer to
Repeat to
Long to
Forget to
— but he is finally
Called on by her
& he can't
Decide whether or no
To her is on
& off many times, finally she
Fury or hatred

———

& that style
In is
In its &
As a matter of fact
But no

———

Over to
To have with
One of my
Him of him
It helped a little
That & his
Use of
Me a lot
Of life etc.
Water under a bridge
Of weeks even months
Than he was
Got a of
It's him into
He has to lose
Go to a, stop, a stop, stop being the

———

Self
Apparently always
Can't have it
Must be because
He can't meet
Other than his
Because he
(Too much for
& can't
To take
But despite all this
Actually very
& caring & this
Was more
Than he'd seemed
We about
& about
Me to him
Which I did

———

We talked about
& the idea of
Poetry as being
As told to
As it had been again
Fury & hatred
Reminding me also
Like the work in
Hebrew
Of the
— which
It does seem to
Be (even
Certainly
Then went on to
At the
She read
The book
The occasion
In
Listening to crows

———

— called "luck"
or more people living with it
in nick of
(That is
From a
Period, very hoary or now
(Through sound
Then she
From some
Speeches by lunatics
I had my
Amazement, despair, refreshment
&
(This is so
So
So
Is a
Among the
Certainly to
Events on the flats, under it
In

———

The depth, originality
Impossible to
More people doing this
She looks
For wear
Now — very long hair
Maybe five or more people living in
Face, face, face
& looking & a day
Me — &
Pants &
No
So she does
Like or like
At end she
Maybe
People
Poorer neighborhoods to to because
Poets
& fretful significance

———

"My first ever" — later
And well I
To have been she or him maybe me
However with such
A soul
Told me, after my
Morning of
That that over of
Daily, one day
Had spoken to him about
Next day
And that the
Of the
Of it
Is best
I could tell
As did
I said the

———

Book too intense
That it took me a
That maybe wasn't
His own songs on guitar
That a young skinny poet
Black or in black
Author of
Shaking woman
In her play
She saw her psyche
In front
You're not supposed to
Written on double expose of
Dolphins swimming
Patterns of moving water maybe waves

———

Husband or wife of
Ideas whereas flesh
Plays on corrupted surfaces
Before died as usual
Then she (in night in
Weekend) in concentrated narration
After died sucked into
Stuck this & that onto it
Fevered
On   &   other
I wanted to do this
So I very old footage
Off at my
For not paying enough attention
We're supposed to be
They tell us
But we're not
My houses are always
I'm a terrible home
— but —
In fact <u>seeing</u>

———

To come to my
Emotional openness
Not all that"
I write I'm afraid
I write a day
I writing coming & unwrite
Going
A plan
Really the essence
A sound
But now I hear
It's almost a
& it becomes the — present
Unfolding of a
Shape in a dark
Mumbled tale
I wanted
To let me sleep
Me
The next
& in
& run together

———

In written while
She ascribed to
High & start
Then got sick & continued
Writing. Depression —
Song in it — that
Respected memory of a friend
As she it
Last summer
In the bathtub
On the
For about as many as
I have
In my — I can go
Listening to
Songs"
You need stuff to sweet little soiree
In back of brain or no not
You have a source
For" in music never heard
Almost

———

"Makes me really
When there's nothing in
I'm always
To put more
In his"
"Of any kind
"There's always
You have to set
Yourself against" : "The
Chair of poetry must re-
Main empty"
"These books
For the . I have to
I don't write for you"
"I gave her all
But I was
She read it"
"When she was
She saw short talk"

———

Quotation in
To get you distort
Like you do
"That's my philosophy : nothing
Stands for anything"
"I don't see
As marks
In my body"
"Do you
of it as a of
Something?"
"No, a poem"
Of Light
Why is that
It [the
Of that] &
It (when
So I knew it was
Important

———

"For rocks & I'm
Animals"
"That began in
That's
Wrong. If we say
That be. All
The same size
For flies!"
"I hate it! It's too
Ethereal. Stress."
For the
Re-typed
Poems from
Early always
Re-typing work
To re-type the
Lines I want to model
Reading of beards

———

Early
This & it
Her to the
Just as
Did to
I do
On paper on floors
To relate to
Writing is cutting up and pasting
That unlock enormous
There is too much
Of came later
Though he was kindness — a non-
For these
She meets a song which
It is quite clear I know nothing
Color sense
"I feel it
& stop"
To express "an object artificial or imagined"
A dramatic sense
Of ending"

———

Returned to the
Center having coffee
Sense of — the
Slays the
Is a plant in
The garden uproots
After having had a cordial meeting
At his house. Since you are
Unreal you can't
So not, it's easy if you don't
(Like that, have
I've already forgotten)
Rather than as a space to reproduce
Great talk on
Stars, the foliage
Up on site
At the
With who

———

Me as an &
But is a
& just as she
Is, very to
But she
Said she
But then we
She knew as
They got to
Because, anyway, it was
But
More, she
Of her
Hope
With her (she
Be in
In me. Funny
Want, need, something from
Me, her, or &

———

Companionship etc.
But I
& it
— or wrecks — too
Important — just
Makes a big
— it's almost
— which I & she
Rolling down from the ocean
Like showers coming down from the sky
Stars
Just from
Me for my
I said I
By the of women
& she said
Men never do. But
It took me time
To appreciate
So obvious — that —

————

& that it
& surprises
"Grief of
The world" I wrote
With rabbi
He has
On what
& I did/are doing
Or — sees it as
To get involved
Or &
But he's
Guy, brilliantly
On &
But therefore
People
Like he
His head in the

———

Clouds to survive (he's
Not get
With madness. But
I told
I was
I/he listened(as they do
How much
About this
He said he felt
Be able to
That — but I
A conceivable way to communicate
To them — that's what
Was to to do
About Heidegger if there is anything
A — his
Right there in
Not from his
(As whoever talks about this must

———

Think — whoever talks
About this listens to talk unspoken
Is think?
— & love but I —
The giant dark gap
In the middle
Does know well
& feels like of
Doesn't go far — that
The is
Whom I've
Book (I have a copy) is
All about &
& its application
A said or saying
Took back this
"No more after the
When they"
In front row of
Several or if not any more than one
At least

———

A young woman appeared
A member of the collective
Three years, the last time at our house
But with weird trembling of limbs
As if in the
Collective anger in
The visionary driving
Was reading itself in her body
Other body tensing it
With stormy mistaken people
Too much hatred art in mistaken people
He thinks in patterning among her many confusing objects

———

My encounter
Just this morning
For my next
For the other one
For always
I feel like the
Of their
— is so
& shining that
(One's own)(others')
Causing doubt
Etc. & thoughts
What I
All the time in
Not enough of
Such any
But go on withal
As if etc
Then the next after that
As normal conditional

———

Better luck next time.
Yes think so.
And thanks.
Yesterday
Event — with &
Heard the
At the
Professional
& bravo and kudos. Good for you
Or them also
Was telling
How smart
How much
In my
& said
Don't" &
I am but
It's simply
As is all
A disadvantage

———

& moaning
Just a simple
Like a boulder
So it rolls heavily
Over & go on
Damaging or reorganizing
My own. Lately
& stuff that
& easy but with
Some rough. Is
All the time I
Them — recent
Gradually graded steep up. &
At night
While, worth, with

———

Just finished
At   in
I get in
— & talks
That I for after
To produce a
Yes I will do that I think so!
Never stop nearly missing that!
Then all
Meal all day. Days. I
Time sheathed & I
Ride the train till
Ending.
In the
Group &
From   from
……from

———

Asian women
Or other sorts
Lots of singing or other confidences
The gardener
Me she
Will be confusing masks
Day this summer
From the up to
Sky she's
Very
But with that
Jumping up eagerly
Entirely connectable
Body
The other is
She up there and between
The & an & a later than
Always been scared of
White men but safe
With & of
Future chapters this one a little too much
(From all the more
Doing it again
As is possible

Near ending
Whole cosmic body
As she showed me
Suddenly my body
& had a hand or leg
Crossing up to limits
Time herself though in it
After which she told of
She'd had
Before she'd
Something failed in the beginning thought
That started rolling
With her infant
In it
In front of the car &
How we should all make preparations
Stories continue a week or so before

———

A of time in
& had a near death
— being surrounded by
Happy to go there
& peace not
About
Not thinking
As dying
The light &
She was lying.
She was telling
I'm glad   it
Was   they expressed
& concern & they
Started an outburst
Along with
Well
This time
She'd lost her mind a
In the . of course
But years
When she read books

———

She the
— that she had
In
Was an
In her
Of longstanding who
At least in my
All
A pretty good
With a few
Not at all
She's a
Over the years
New to in
Of
To
&
As if
With. But

———

I know there's nothing
To me the fact
No doubt
Who are not
I suppose it's
For
Who are
& want — &
Opposite of this
In need of
Time presenting me with
&
— who went
Sham ceremony
In noisy silence
But sincere
As had as needed
As anyone would
That it had
As — & heard
That
What happened was

———

"An un-
This & she
It as a
She said "I'm
From you
From this" As if
& is
Before I can be
In my needful time
But I said, Well I
To a
That when
I'll do
Before it
If I have to and if it it & it
No, possibly if
— or like
Colorful
& living in their own world

———

Who knows — it
But I guess
I must have
With that
Too much
But, at that
Time, had barely
Had been such
Help
So I was
Of control
Good thing
She went away when
She did.
Have made the
We now
And that was

———

Her & everyone
From there. But
Had an epiphany — that she
Had failed a
& also (as I did)
Her in her   by
So, yes, it's
Not just the last moment child
To keep — it's
Of the month or week
Which I & rely
On.
Also these
There's — unknowably —
Much going on
Onto
Me that
& shouldn't possess

———

Came into &
Talked
About
Such
An odd little anyone
Probably as of
Somehow. He said
Working on a wizard
A miracle right now
Where else?
I don't always have to
How smart I am every time
But in fact
Making a
Witty joke
Answering the unwritten question
Jumping up
Like he really wants
This momentary living
Animated by ink

———

As soon as
— & why not? But this time
He would say — & oddly said
As he was
Of course leaving
That he swept up and threw away the ball
He was out of control
But seemed
Then said
But then said
But later realized
Or was
A certain way on the
It certain
Which cause of hidden causes
And think how he said
That as he
This year as never before
Didn't & last
Year & powerful

———

Very sad to hear those names
Of those just dead &
To him. But
Dead this year —
Lots
From this & other
Close ones loved ones always someones
Crowded in heaven
More people there
Friend — I
My talk words float off
Morning evening night
People
Their dead &
Receive them
Wherever they go
Afterward
A powerful
Transcendence gets misplaced

———

His parents
& hadn't
Always breached
At a buried point
Suddenly he said
He felt a forgiveness
A body wanting its settled place
Mental gratitude suffusing
Broad-minded in its way surprising
Which he realized
Altered reality
Scope. The
Parent-shape
In religion
The affection & pain &
Stand-in
With the
Memory before walking
There's then walking
Automatic

———

(Very basic)
For disturbing experiences
Lots of
Disappointed —
Seven days in week seven beggars on street
First part
As bad as the last
Personal details
Sheathed
Aways one's own persuasively
Therefore God
Demands surfaces
To deny is basest & best
Atheist God in face of
Everyday experience
Possessed by zeitgeist
In basic interpretation

———

& funny & people
(much longer than
any)
Games of
Were during the
To watch
Of the earlier
& eating too
Were so intense
& disturbing for so
Soon ended
With a performance
Who has been
Almost in the post-
(Though he's no or
Even early
Who had
Doesn't that a
Have — yet

———

So
Was a lock & went
Back to ahead to
But
Already in &
Against
Who used to be a
Good & now once
Is. This left with
For   who
Also used to be a
But usually lately isn't
He lasted maybe & with
The in the
Put in on
Days rest, the rest
Of the   on a basis   &

Wish I
But more or less
In between
Suns.
Practice
Two, one,
Mind about
Her life as a child of
The other on
Both very simple &
(She's got a
& is a)
& everyone
To compete with
Year.
The was
& by me
Came to talk

———

To me about
I didn't entirely
Seemed to be
I had the
Following the game or talking
Others didn't
But somehow the point
Remained oddly obscure
That this is
& that
Probably her
With larger-than-life life
Who jumped off
Comes in
With great
& a feeling of
That I understand

———

& then at the end
As if an act
Honest &
Must be said
Our good relationship
Up some
And say something like
"Well I am
Like this."
Very intricate!
This morning cloud
Quite intricate
About his
& how he &
& happier
with the
(that's going on with
& a new location)

———

I can understand.
It doesn't
Have to feel
A problem belonging to her
Or solved or defined —
Or lack of
More defined
Got her of she's
Into those
Who came
To the at an
Of its are going to
As &
Do, maybe too
(Is me but
Never mentions).

———

Not wanting to talk
So don't say
That is just
Not really a
Usually, even if
Life's
Still dark, but at least
Out   of   in
In.   I worry
To get over all
& get on
But not
Well, maybe it's all
A mess
But she's
She has to
She says OK
Very elegant

———

Despite the
She thinks
In it — metaphorical —
That someone
Could think
Actually not
Spatially but it's not
That someone thinks
All is well but
Somehow you
When this is
I haven't
Been honest
In speaking but
Yes
Even in lying about fact
All cards on
Table

———

Night &
Rain. That doesn't
No steering
Finally I get it to
(If I persist) I'm
Going from but
— I don't
Know how — but, again
Wearing out
Sleeping in —
— a group
Of people cards
At a table
— not real —
Person comes out
Upstairs room
Floats downstairs
Brothers shout,
Leaving

———